Why the Glory of God Through the Church Will Soon Shake the World

THE
COMING
GLORY

Peter John Brooks

THE COMING GLORY: Why the Glory of God Through the Church Will Soon Shake the World

Print ISBN: 978-1-968804-09-1

Digital ISBN: 978-1-968804-08-4

Published by Fivestone New Media

www.bethelcornerstone.org

Contents

The Lord will arise over you, and his glory will be seen upon you.

Isaiah 60:2b

David was not a believer in the theory that the world will grow worse and worse, and that the dispensation will wind up with general darkness and idolatry. Earth's sun is to go down amid tenfold night if some of our prophetic brethren are to be believed. Not so do we expect, but we look for a day when the dwellers in all lands shall learn righteousness, shall trust in the Saviour, shall worship thee alone, O God, and shall glorify thy name. The modern notion has greatly damped the zeal of the church for missions, and the sooner it is shown to be unscriptural, the better for the cause of God. It neither consorts with prophecy, honors God, nor inspires the church with ardor. Far hence be it driven.

Charles Haddon Spurgeon, *Treasury of David*

Introduction

IT'S TIME to re-think the end times.

Before you read this book, pray and ask God to teach you his truth. Jesus said the Holy Spirit will lead his people into all truth (John 16:13).

The glory of God defines the future of the world. The glory of God is coming, and nothing will be able to stop it.

It's time to view the end times in the light of God's glory.

1

The Glorious Plan

GOD HAS A GREAT PLAN for his people. In the end of this age, they will rise up and actually embrace all that Jesus bought for them when he died on the cross and rose again. Their divine inheritance will become a reality, not just a theology, and they will begin to reveal God's kingdom, power, and glory into the earth. The Bible promises that "the earth will be filled with the knowledge of the glory of the Lord, as the waters cover the sea" (Habakkuk 2:14). This will happen through the church, God's redeemed nation.

These great things are not just for a heavenly time in the future when we're all floating around on clouds with Jesus strumming harps. These things are for now, for this earth, for you and me – if we will seize the kingdom of God. Jesus said the violent seize the kingdom (Matthew 11:12). Now is the time for spiritual violence; now is the time for radical souls to seize the kingdom of God.

It's time for "the people who know their God [to] be strong and carry out great exploits" (Daniel 11:32).

God's creation is going to be redeemed. His glory is going to be revealed. His power will be made known. Sin and sickness will be history. Death will be destroyed. It is not so now, but it will be soon.

Vision

Vision creates possibilities; it produces forward movement. What we see is what we can begin to walk into. Without vision, the way is dark. When we can't see, we can't move forward. "Where there is no vision, the people perish" (Proverbs 29:18, KJV). Without vision, there is stagnation and ultimately death. We need vision; we need to see where we're going.

As Christians, we are called to enter into a future that is defined by God. We need spiritual vision in order to enter into the things God has for us. When we can see new things, we can experience those things. We must pioneer the way into the future that God defines, and not be held back by our own fears or the lies of culture around us. The expansiveness of our spiritual vision will largely determine the extent of our experience of God.

> *The expansiveness of our vision will largely determine the extent of our experience of God.*

The glory of God is coming soon, and it's time to see the possibilities. We need to stop looking at ourselves and our own limitations, and look to the one who created the universe.

Jesus is the name above all names. He has conquered death, shed his blood to rescue us, and lives today in our hearts. All authority in heaven and earth is given to him. There is no power in the universe greater than Jesus. When Christ dominates our field of vision, our faith will increase, and this will open the door for God to move.

The Loss of Glory

In the beginning, the world was perfect. Adam, Eve, and God were in perfect union. The plants and animals were in perfect harmony. The universe sang praise to Almighty God, and glory was all over the world.

Out from the midst of this perfect tableau fell a powerful angel who became Satan. He turned into a snake, slithered into the Garden, and tricked Adam and Eve. The primeval couple rejected God, fell into sin, and enthroned Satan as "god of this age" (2 Corinthians 4:4).

The gates of hell were opened. Evil flooded in. Paradise was lost. Death reigned. The plants and animals were corrupted. God's beautiful creation that he had pronounced "Very good!" became horribly twisted.

Sin ravaged the world. "All have sinned and fall short of the glory of God" (Romans 3:23). A better translation is: "all have sinned and lack the glory of God". Sin caused humanity and the creation to lack God's glory.

This was not the end of the story. God was not going to allow Satan's claws to permanently mar his masterpiece.

Jesus took up the challenge. Like a strong warrior, he came down from heaven, determined to set the creation free from the grip of the serpent. He came to demolish sin, destroy death, and reverse the curse. He came to restore God's masterful creation to pristine splendor and bring glory back to the world.

When Jesus was born in Bethlehem, the powerful work of redemption began.

Redeemed for Glory

Reconciliation involves sacrifice. Jesus was born in disreputable circumstances in an animal feeding trough. He died an inglorious death at the hands of sinners, tortured and executed as a common criminal. Heaven's mighty warrior endured unspeakable humiliation and shame.

But through apparent defeat, Jesus won. By yielding to injustice, Jesus did away with injustice; by submitting to death, he destroyed it. By going to the cross, Jesus ushered in redemptive possibilities for mankind and for the entire creation. Because he came like a baby and died like a sinner, we, in spite of our inability, could be saved. His weakness became our glory.

Jesus could have come to Earth another way. He could have arrived from the skies in glorious light and blazed forth the glory of God. But such divine brightness would have brought destruction to an unredeemed world, turning a corrupt world to ashes.

This is why the Son of God was shrouded by humanity. It's why he laid his glory aside. Love caused him to take on human flesh.

While he lived on Earth, Jesus did mighty miracles and spoke powerful words. He revealed God's glory (John 2:11). But Jesus did not walk in the full potential of glory. If he had, the age would have ended in a flash of blinding light. Instead, Jesus laid aside God's glory, went to the cross, and died. He brought redemption for the world, went back to Heaven, and poured out the Holy Spirit. Then he "sat down at the right hand of God, from that time waiting till his enemies are made his footstool" (Hebrews 10:12b-13). Christ redeemed the world so that it can shine forth the glory of God, as God originally intended.

What Is Glory?

Glory is not easy to define.

In Hebrew, glory is *kabod,* which means *weight.* It is something heavy. When the glory of God comes, other, lighter things are displaced. Glory is something that makes an impact; it makes an imprint. Glory leaves a mark.

In Greek, glory is *doxa,* which means *shining* or *famous.* Glory is something bright that will not be hidden. God's glory is what makes God famous. It is brighter than the noonday sun. Glory is the outshining of the invisible, eternal God, so he can be seen, known, and enjoyed.

Glory is the ultimate goal of God in creating the world, according to theologians like Jonathan Edwards, who wrote the stunning book *The End for Which God Created the World.* God created the world so that his glory can be revealed and enjoyed by his creatures. The Westminster Catechism says, "man's chief end is to glorify God and to enjoy Him forever."

> Glory is God's ultimate goal in creating the world.

Glut Yourself on Glory

We were made to glorify God. When we glorify God, we fulfill our ultimate purpose. We need God's glory for our own health and sanity. There is nothing that can satisfy us like the glory of God. As John Piper famously said, "God is most glorified in us when we are most satisfied in Him."

Let's starve ourselves from lesser things so we can feast on the glory of God.

C.S. Lewis says,

> It would seem that Our Lord finds our desires not too strong, but too weak. We are half-hearted creatures, fooling about with drink and sex and ambition when infinite joy is offered us, like an ignorant child who wants to go on making mud pies in a slum because he cannot imagine what is meant by the offer of a holiday at the sea. We are far too easily pleased. (Lewis, *The Weight of Glory, and Other Addresses*)

When we enjoy our awesome God, we revel in his glory. This makes us truly glad, and it gives genuine praise to God. When we really appreciate something, we will genuinely praise it. It's easy to praise something we like. When we see how awesome God is (and he truly is awesome), praise will ring out from us as a natural expression of a heart struck by the wonder and majesty of God. When we are ravished with the glory of God, we will fulfill our divine purpose and experience true joy.

Where Is the Glory?

In eternity past, God's glory was in and with God. The glory of the Godhead rested in the Son, who is "the brightness of [God's] glory" (Hebrews 1:3).

Glory was briefly reflected in the earth at the creation of the world, but the terrestrial glory was lost when Adam sinned.

Although glory left the earth after the Fall, Jesus still had glory up in heaven. He could have remained there, shining out the glory of God for eternity.

But he didn't. Two thousand years ago, Jesus laid aside his glory and came to earth in a virgin's womb. After growing into manhood and teaching humanity God's way, Jesus died and rose up again, redeeming the world. Then we went to heaven and received the glory back that he had with the Father from the foundation of the world (John 17:5).

Then Jesus did an amazing thing. He gave the glory away. "The glory which you gave me I have given to them" (John 17:22a).

This statement is in the past tense: "have given." It has already happened. Jesus gave his glory to his people. He died to share God's glory. His death on the cross opened up the way for people, through faith, to possess the glory of God. His body was broken and his blood was shed so that we could become members of his body (Ephesians 5:30). Joined with him, we become co-heirs of God. We are "heirs of God, and joint-heirs with

> *The cross made a way for people to possess the glory of God.*

Christ" (Romans 8:17b). Jesus' inheritance has become our inheritance. The glory of God is now the possession of the church, the holy company of the redeemed.

This is stupendous - we have the glory of God now! Perhaps the full meaning of this has yet to sink in. It's possible to possess something wonderful but never use it. Someone may have the most powerful tool in the world, but if he doesn't know how to operate it, it will just sit on the shelf.

We "plead with you not to receive the grace of God in vain" (2 Corinthians 6:1b).

It's possible to receive a wonderful gift from God, but not do anything with it. It's possible to receive a huge inheritance, but never cash the check.

Glory Is Coming

We are approaching God's appointed time. The glorious purpose of Jesus' redemption is about to be revealed for the world to see. The glory of God is coming, and nothing can stop it.

> For the earth will be filled with the knowledge of the glory of the Lord, as the water covers the sea. (Habakkuk 2:14)

God's glory is going to fill the earth. Everyone will see it and know about it. Glory will transform the world, and God will be exalted over everything.

Let's be confident in the coming glory.

F.B. Meyer said, "that the age would close with a worldwide Pentecost" (A.J. Gordon, *The Ministry of the Spirit*).

C.H. Spurgeon said, "I see no reason why we should not have a greater Pentecost than Peter saw" (*Sermon, April 19, 1874*).

D.L. Moody said, "Another great work of the Holy Spirit, which is not accomplished, is the bringing on of the latter-day glory. In a few more years - I know not when, I know not how - the Holy Spirit will be poured out in a far different style from the present (Moody, *Holy Ghost*).

God's saints throughout history have known this: in the last days the Holy Spirit will be poured on his people in an unprecedented way. This is inevitable, for the word of God says it will happen. And when the Holy Spirit comes, God's glory is revealed.

God said, "it shall come to pass afterward that I will pour out My Spirit on all flesh; your sons and your daughters shall prophesy" (Joel 2:28).

Isaiah said, "the glory of the Lord shall be revealed, and all flesh shall see it together; for the mouth of the Lord has spoken" (Isa. 40:5).

The angels around God's throne prophetically speak glory into the earth - all the time, every moment of every day. "Holy, holy, holy is the Lord of hosts; the whole earth is full of His glory!" (Isa. 6:3). This prophetic declaration controls the future of the world.

We are approaching the end of the age. The redemption of Jesus has been at work in the earth for 2,000 years. Redemption and reconciliation through Jesus' blood have been paving the way for God's glory to be revealed. The creation is about to fulfill its purpose. The end result of Christ's sacrifice is about to be revealed.

How will God's glory arrive?

God is not going to dump glory down onto the world with powerful angels and sudden power. He's not just going to snap his fingers and say, "Glory Time!" and astound everyone.

God works through people. Moses built the Tabernacle, Solomon built the temple; both became habitations of God's glory. Noah built a boat - the means of salvation for the entire world. God didn't build these things; men did, working with God. When God works on the earth, he does so through people who hear his voice and do what he says.

We have a responsibility. Through Adam the creation lost the glory. Through the power of Jesus, the people of God will recover the glory. He's already given us power. It's time to act. When the Holy Spirit is poured out, and God's people live as God intends, the creation will once again fulfill the glorious purpose for which it was made - to glorify Almighty God.

- *Points to Ponder* -

1. The world was made for the glory of God.

2. The world lost the glory of God when Adam sinned.

3. Jesus came to deliver the world from evil and restore the glory of God to the world.

4. God's glory is the only thing that can truly satisfy us.

5. Jesus gave God's glory to his people. We are called to reveal his glory to the world.

6. Someday God's glory will be restored to the world.

- *Prayer* -

Heavenly Father, thank you for creating this world to reveal your glory. You made everything for yourself and for your praise. Though this world was broken, it's going to be healed. You are going to glorify yourself through your creation. Open my eyes to see your glory. Help me turn away from the things of the world and focus my appetite upon you. As I study your glory, help me understand. Teach me by your Holy Spirit. Deliver me from all deception. Give me faith to believe in the glorious possibilities that exist because of your Son Jesus Christ. In his name I pray. Amen.

2

The House of God

Lord, I have loved the habitation of Your house, and the
place where Your glory dwells.

Psalm 26:8

THE HOUSE OF GOD PRECEDES the manifestation of
God's glory. If we're going to experience God's glory, we
must first discover his house. God's house is the place
where God dwells. Where God dwells, his glory is revealed.

History will culminate in the full revelation of the glory
of God all over the world. This means that history is
waiting for a clear and full manifestation of the house of

God. When God's house is built according to God's word, there can be a full manifestation of his glory.

Tabernacle of Moses

Moses was the first person who built a house for God. This first house was the tabernacle, a mobile tent made of animal skins and cloth. When the tabernacle was finished, God's glory came into it.

> So Moses finished the work. Then the cloud covered the tabernacle of meeting, and the glory of the Lord filled the tabernacle. And Moses was not able to enter the tabernacle of meeting, because the cloud rested above it, and the glory of the Lord filled the tabernacle. (Exodus 40:33b-35)

The tabernacle became the dwelling-place of God. When people wanted to meet with God, they came to the tabernacle. When they wanted to serve God, they did so at the tabernacle. The tabernacle was God's first house on the earth, and it became the seat of his glory.

Temple

Centuries later, Solomon built God a temple. This temple at Jerusalem was made of wood and stone. When the temple was completed, God's glory came into it.

And it came to pass, when the priests came out of the holy place, that the cloud filled the house of the Lord, so that the priests could not continue ministering because of the cloud; for the glory of the Lord filled the house of the Lord. (1 Kings 8:10-11)

The glory of God had moved out from the tabernacle into the temple.

Jesus Christ

Centuries later, Jesus Christ came. He said, "destroy this temple, and in three days I will raise it up'... He was speaking of the temple of His body" (John 2:19-21).

When Jesus was filled with the Holy Spirit, he became God's house on the earth. The glory of God moved out from the Jerusalem temple into the physical body of Jesus Christ.

Jesus brought the glory of God into the world in a greater way than the tabernacle or the temple. When people met and touched Jesus, they met and touched God. When they saw Jesus, they saw God. Jesus said, "he who has seen Me has seen the Father (John 14:9b).

Jesus was the point at which God touched the earth - the place where heaven and earth intersected. Whenever Jesus taught, God spoke through him. Whenever Jesus did a miracle, God worked through him. The words and works of God flowed through Jesus into the earth. Jesus was the interface between earth and heaven, a temple where people met God, worshiped God, and served God.

Jesus astounded the world with a revelation of God's glory, bringing life, healing, and salvation wherever he went. He cast out demons, healed the sick, and raised the dead. Things like that never occurred at the tabernacle of Moses or the temple in Jerusalem.

Jesus is "the brightness of His glory" (Heb. 1:3). As the perfect house of God, Jesus perfectly showed forth the glory of God.

Jesus was God's house as God originally intended— a human house. "The Most High does not dwell in temples made with hands" (Acts 7:48). God had always wanted to dwell in people, not in buildings. But because of sin, he was unable to dwell in human hearts. Jesus was perfect. This meant that the Holy Spirit could dwell inside of Jesus in fullness.

> Jesus was the true Bethel. He was God's house as originally intended.

Jesus, the living house of God, lived by the power of God's glory inside him. He could become invisible

(John 8:59). He could knock down violent mobs with a word (John 18:6). His body could be transported from one place to another by spiritual means. He knew secrets. He knew the future. He even rose from the dead. After that, he walked through walls, floated through the sky, and did many other things. Jesus was not confined by natural laws because he lived in the Father who created the universe, and the Father lived in him.

But rather than tread on the earth in blazing light all by himself, Jesus died. Through death, Jesus reconciled the world to God.

"God was in Christ, reconciling the world to Himself" (2 Corinthians 5:19b).

His blood took away sin. After his resurrection, he went back to heaven and poured out the Holy Spirit, unshackling people from the limitations of their flesh and bringing them into the limitless power and possibilities of the Holy Spirit.

The Disciples Become Temples of God

Christ's sacrifice turned all those who believe in him into the temples of God.

"Do you not know that your body is the temple of the Holy Spirit who is in you, whom you have from God?" (1 Corinthians 6:19a).

The Holy Spirit dwells inside each believer in Jesus. This means that each believer is a house of God. Today, there are many temples of God on Earth. These are human temples, like Jesus was. They are mobile. They can go into almost any place on Earth, create an open window in Heaven, and release God's glory.

The same Holy Spirit that raised up Jesus from the dead is inside us. This means that we can do the same works Jesus did.

"Most assuredly, I say to you, he who believes in Me, the works that I do, he will do also; and greater works than these he will do" (John 14:12a).

The powerful Holy Spirit who is inside us has already conquered it all. He destroyed sin, conquered death, defeated Satan, and removed the curse. Jesus died and rose again so we can experience the many-splendored facets of God's glory. Miracles, demon-busting power, authority over sin and sickness, even victory over death, are all parts of our glorious inheritance in God.

We are called to be like Jesus. As he was God's temple, releasing God's glory into the world, so are we.

"Christ in you [is] the hope of glory" (Colossians 1:27).

Christ inside his people is the hope that the world will experience God's glory. The glory of God is already inside us. We need to let the glory out. God wants his glory released. The internal glory must become an external reality. Glory must shape our relationships and circumstances. It must shape the world.

The Church Is God's Temple

There's more. Not only are we as individual believers the temples of God, but the worldwide church is the massive worldwide temple of God.

> In whom the whole building, being fitted together, grows into a holy temple in the Lord, in whom you also are being built together for a dwelling place of God in the Spirit. (Ephesians 2:21-22)

Peter said, "you also, as living stones, are being built up a spiritual house" (1 Peter 2:5). Each believer in Jesus is a living stone that is being built up with other believers into a vast temple of God. This huge building, comprised of believers all over the world, is the grand temple of God on Earth today.

The church is Christ's body. This familiar fact is packed with meaning. We are the hands and feet of Jesus on Earth. All authority in Heaven and on Earth has been given to him (Matthew 28:18). "As he is, so are we in this world" (1 John 4:17b). Jesus is glorified in Heaven and has all authority. We are called to be like him - to manifest his power and glory to the world.

> And He put all things under His feet, and gave Him to be head over all things to the church, which is His body, the fullness of Him who fills all in all. (Ephesians 1:22-23)

God is working in the Earth through His church. He is acting through His church and speaking through His church.

"I will dwell in them and walk among them. I will be their God, and they shall be My people" (2 Corinthians 6:16b).

Individual believers have the Holy Spirit inside them. They are little temples that can release the glory of God in measure. The church is a massive temple that will be able to release God's glory in fullness. The church is God's final house on Earth through which He is ultimately going to impact the

The church is God's final house on earth.

32

entire world with His glory.

It is possible for God's glory to cover the earth. God is inside us, we are all over the world, and with God all things are possible. In every nation, God wants His glory to break out. This means that the church will someday fulfill her calling and release the glory of God all over the world. When this happens, the age will be over.

Church History and Destiny

The temple in Jerusalem is a symbol of the church. This temple went through three main stages.

1. The temple was built and filled with God's glory.
2. Through disobedience, the glory was lost, the temple was destroyed, and the Israelites went into captivity in Babylon.
3. Years later, Israel returned to Jerusalem and the temple was rebuilt. Then the glory returned, and Jesus Christ came into the temple.

The church is going through three similar stages.

1. In the first century, the church was built into a glorious state by the apostles.
2. After this, the church fell from God into disobedience. For about 1,000 years, from 500-1500, the

church was in spiritual darkness in Babylon. The glory was lost.

3. Since about AD 1500, the church is being rebuilt. The Reformation sparked the recovery of truth to the church. First, the doctrine of salvation by grace through faith was restored through men like Martin Luther. Holiness was recovered through people like John Wesley. Baptism of believers in water was recovered by the Anabaptists. The baptism of the Holy Spirit and the spiritual gifts were recovered at the turn of the 20th century by other truth pioneers. Step by step, the powerful truths of Jesus are still being restored to the church. Eventually, the church will be completely rebuilt, and she will be filled with glory.

The history of the temple in Jerusalem and the history of the church are the same: glory, then apostasy, then glory.

We live in a time of the third stage. The church is being rebuilt. We must dedicate ourselves to edifying or building up the church as God desires the church to be, if we want to see the fullness of God's glory revealed to the world.

D. Martyn-Lloyd Jones said this:

My dear friends, here is the great need of the hour. It is not merely that we should perpetuate a denomination or an organization or an institution. No, no! It is for Christians to become the living church of Christ, filled with his life and power, charged with the energy of the Spirit divine, and standing as a phenomenon in this modern, evil world. (Lloyd-Jones, *Setting Our Affections upon Glory: Nine Sermons on the Gospel and the Church*)

The church is rebuilt as truth is recovered. When the fullness of the word of God is embraced by God's people, the church will be rebuilt. She will stand on the earth in the full intention of what God wants her to be. Then she will reveal God's glory to the world. The glory of the end-times church will be greater than the glory of the early church.

"The glory of this latter temple shall be greater than the former" (Hag. 2:9).

To this rebuilt temple, Jesus Christ will come again.

The Bride of Christ

The church is called to be the bride of Christ. Jesus is waiting for his bride to get ready for him. He's waiting for "a glorious church, not having spot, or wrinkle, or any such thing, but that it should be holy and without blemish" (Ephesians 5:27b). Jesus wants to get married, and for that to happen, his church must be ready.

The church is called to be full of God's glory. To become glorious, we don't need to wait for God to zap us with heavenly whitening powder and detergent. Jesus has already shed his blood, poured out his Spirit, and given us the Bible. We don't need anything more. On the cross, he said, "It's finished!" (John 19:30). Jesus has done all that needs to be done to equip us to fulfill our calling. It's our responsibility to take the things Jesus has already given us and get ready for him.

Jesus is waiting for his bride to prepare herself and, through the word of God, become his glorious counterpart on Earth. He's waiting for his house to be completed. God is waiting for us more than we are waiting for him. No amount of pining for God will bring the final outpouring of the Spirit without our obedient preparation.

> *No amount of pining for God will bring the final outpouring of the Holy Spirit without our obedient preparation.*

The only way the bride can be prepared is through submission to the word of God. We must be willing to abandon the empty religious traditions of people and completely yield to God's word, not loving our lives unto death. God's house must be built in God's way, and then the glory will come.

"The marriage of the lamb has come, and his wife has made herself ready" (Revelation 19:7b).

She *made herself ready* - she took responsibility for what needed to be done, and by the power of the Spirit of God, she did it.

At the end of the age, when the church is ready, Jesus will come into her by his Spirit and fill her with glory. His bride will be glorious. Then the glory of God will overflow both the individual bodies of believers and the worldwide church of God, and spill out from his people into the world. The earth will be transformed.

- Points to Ponder -

1. The house of God is the place where God dwells on Earth. Through God's house, his glory is to be revealed to the world.

2. Today, the house of God on Earth is the church.

3. The church is the bride of Christ. At the end of the age, the Bible says that the church will be glorious.

4. Through the church, the glory of God will come into the world.

Dear God, thank you for revealing your plans through your word. Help me to understand the awesome privileges and responsibilities I have as a temple of the Holy Spirit. I am learning that I cannot fulfill my purpose apart from the Biblical church, which is your glorious house on Earth. Deliver me from all misconceptions about the church. Help me to find other believers who seek to conform to your word. Help me to leave all man-made religious traditions behind. Help me to make the sacrifices necessary to be a part of your glorious bride. In the name of Jesus, I pray. Amen.

3

The Sons of God

The Church exists for nothing else but to draw men into Christ, to make them little Christs. If they are not doing that, all the cathedrals, clergy, missions, sermons, even the Bible itself are simply a waste of time. God became Man for no other purpose. It is even doubtful, you know, whether the whole universe was created for any other purpose.... The Son of God became a man to enable men to become sons of God.

C.S. Lewis, *Mere Christianity*

JESUS IS the only begotten Son of God. But one son wasn't enough for God. He wanted more. So the Father sent Jesus to Earth to rescue people, cleanse them, fill them with Himself, and transform them into His sons. Jesus conquered death, reconciled man to God, and made it possible for us to become like Him.

"For you are all sons of God through faith in Christ Jesus" (Galatians 3:26).

When we believe in Jesus, we become the sons of God. As sons of God, we have a new identity. We are no longer slaves of sin, blind to God, and under judgment. We become new creations through Christ. We become slaves of righteousness and ambassadors of God - the temples of God on Earth. Praise God for our new identity as the sons of God.

"As many as received Him, to them He gave power to become the sons of God" (John 1:12a KJV).

Along with a new identity, God has given us power. It takes spiritual power to walk on earth as a son of God. God gave us the power of sonship. As we appropriate the spiritual treasures that God freely gives us, who we are as the sons of God defines us more and more, and we begin to actually walk as Jesus walked.

Sonship is more than a reflection of parentage. It is a reflection of nature, status, and inheritance. The potential of a son is related to the power, character, wealth, and authority of his father. And if the Father is the King who created and owns the universe, to be his son is absolutely amazing.

God wants us to become mature. He doesn't want us to be baby Christians our whole life.

God wants us to keep growing until we fulfill our destiny, which is to become like his Son Jesus. This is the reason he's given us the power of sonship - so this can actually happen. God doesn't stop at half-measures. He goes all out. He wants people who are fully redeemed, co-heirs with Jesus of his glory. God wants his glory shared. He wants many heirs. He wants a lot of children who are walking on the earth as representatives of their Father.

> *God doesn't want us to remain baby Christians. He wants us to mature. That's why he's given us power.*

Jesus came to bring "many sons to glory" (Hebrews 2:10). He didn't just come to call them sons. He came to *make* them sons. He came to bring them to glory. He gave them spiritual power to become like himself.

"For whom He foreknew, He also predestined to be conformed to the image of His Son, that He might be the firstborn among many brethren (Romans 8:29).

God has chosen us to be like Jesus. This is the reason God has chosen us. It's what we've been preordained for from the foundation of the world.

The Grain of Wheat - the Death of One Son Produces Many More

"Most assuredly, I say to you, unless a grain of wheat falls into the ground and dies, it remains alone; but if it dies, it produces much grain" (John 12:24).

When a grain of wheat is planted into the ground, the seed falls apart. It loses its wholeness as a seed. The shell is broken, and the seed sort of dissolves. It dies. But through death, the seed rises again and becomes something new - a sprout. As time goes on, this sprout grows to become a plant. When the plant is mature, it produces many grains. These mature wheat grains look very similar to the original grain that was initially planted into the ground.

This is an important symbolic picture.

Jesus is the seed of God, "the seed of the woman" (Genesis 3:15). He died on the cross and was buried, planted in the earth. Then he rose from the dead, birthing the church. The church is like God's plant. The church, the body of Christ, is currently growing into maturity, into "a perfect man, the measure of the stature of the fullness of Christ" (Ephesians 4:13).

When the church reaches maturity, she will produce fruit. The fruit of the church will be the mature sons of God. These "grains" will look remarkably similar to Jesus, the original "Grain" sown into the earth 2,000 years ago. The sons of God are the harvest that God is waiting for.

Growing Into Maturity

When we are born again, we become the sons of God. But we are not suddenly revealed to the world in all our full potential as the sons of God. We must mature.

The way that we mature is to see more of Jesus. As we get a greater revelation of Christ, we become more and more like him.

> Beloved, now are we the sons of God; and it doth not yet appear what we shall be: but we know that, when he shall appear, we shall be like him; for we shall see him as he is. (1 John 3:2 KJV)

As we see Jesus, we are transformed into his image. We become like him. When we see him in fullness, then we will be conformed into his image. This process is happening now.

J.C. Ryle said, "he that would be conformed to Christ's image, and become a Christ-like man, must be constantly studying Christ Himself" (J.C. Ryle, *Holiness: Its Nature, Hindrances, Difficulties, and Roots*).

As we study Jesus, we see more of who he is, and then we become like him. This is the way to maturity! He is our goal. As we see more of Christ, who we are as sons of God defines us more and more.

> The way to maturity is seeing more of Jesus.

> But we all, with unveiled face, beholding as in a mirror the glory of the Lord, are being transformed into the same image from glory to glory, just as by the Spirit of the Lord. (2 Corinthians 3:18)

The veil has been removed from our face so that we are able to see Jesus as he is. As we see him, we are transformed into his image. This process is happening now. The Holy Spirit is transforming us from one degree of glory to a higher degree of glory.

Be Fully Mature

The goal of the Christian life is to become like Christ. Christ is perfect.

"Therefore you shall be perfect, just as your Father in heaven is perfect" (Matthew 5:48).

Jesus commanded us to be as perfect as his Father is. This is not an option, it's a command.

Don't be scared by the word *perfect*. The New Testament uses the word *perfect* differently than we do in English. In Greek the word perfect is *teleios* which means to be fully grown, or fully mature.

Jesus is "the author and finisher of our faith" (Hebrews 12:2). The word *finisher* is *perfecter* (*teleios*). Jesus began working on us, and he is still working on us to finish (or perfect) what he started. He wants us to become *perfect* or *mature*. This is God's will. It's what God is doing within us. As we keep looking to Jesus, we mature. This is not up to our own strength. It's up to Jesus. He's going to finish what he started.

"He who has begun a good work in you will complete it (*teleios*) until the day of Jesus Christ" (Philippians 1:6).

Jesus died to bring full redemption to humanity. He is the captain of our salvation, the forerunner who entered into God's presence on our behalf. He tore the thick veil that separated humanity from God, and he made it possible for us to partake of God's fullness.

"And Jesus cried out with a loud voice, and breathed His last. Then the veil of the temple was torn in two from top to bottom" (Mark 15:47-48).

Jesus gives us access into God's presence through His blood.

> Therefore, brethren, [we have] boldness to enter the Holiest by the blood of Jesus, by a new and living way which He consecrated for us, through the veil, that is, His flesh. (Hebrews 10:19-20)

We can come boldly into God's presence. As we do, we partake of God in increasing measure. This causes us to mature.

The Revelation of the Sons of God

Paul summed up the history and future of the world in the following passage in Romans.

> For I consider that the sufferings of this present time are not worthy to be compared with the glory which shall be revealed in us. For the earnest expectation of the creation eagerly waits for the revealing of the sons of God. For the creation was subjected to futility, not willingly, but because of Him who subjected it in hope; because the creation itself also will be delivered from the bondage of corruption into

the glorious liberty of the children of God. (Romans 8:18-21)

The creation was made to glorify God. At the beginning, it did, as everything was perfect and reflected God's life, peace, and joy. But since the Fall, the creation has been subject to decay, corruption, and the curse. Instead of reflecting the glory of God, it has been groaning under the pain of sin and death. For thousands of years, the creation has been subject to futility, not fulfilling the purpose for which God made it. The creation is longing to be free from evil so that it can once again fulfill its glorious purpose.

The creation is not waiting for angels to clean up the world. It's not waiting for Jesus to come back. Romans 8:19 says the creation is waiting for the revelation of the sons of God, because they will set the creation free from corruption. The sons of God are people like you and me. They are people who are filled with the glory of God.

The glory of God is not something that will just be released from heaven, dumped on the world like a mighty flood. Paul says it will be revealed *to us* (see Greek, Romans 8:18). *Us* is God's people who are alive on the earth. Great glory will come to God's people, transforming them. Then the glory will flow like a spiritual torrent *through* God's people into the world. The sons of God will release glory that will set the creation free.

When we become mature in Christ, we will be filled with glory, and we will be like Jesus. When we walk in our full spiritual potential on earth, the world will see us as we actually are - the sons of God.

When the sons of God are revealed on the earth, they will shine forth God's glory and power. The revelation of glory through them will set the creation free from corruption.

When glory of God comes, the earth itself will be changed. "The creation itself also will be delivered from the bondage of corruption into the glorious liberty of the children of God" (Romans 8:21).

In that glorious day, the plants and animals will be changed. Lions will lie down with lambs. Carnivores will eat straw like oxen (Isaiah 11:6-9 and 65:25). Poisonous plants and thorny bushes will be replaced with milder varieties (Isaiah 55:13). Death will be cast out of the world, and the earth will be set free from the bondage of corruption.

The revelation of the sons of God hasn't happened yet. It hadn't happened in Paul's day, for in his apostolic prime he said the creation was still waiting for it. It hadn't happened later in the first century after Paul wrote Romans, for at that time the church had fallen into apostasy, not risen to glory. The revelation of the sons of God will happen at the end of the age, when Jesus returns to the earth.

David Wilkerson, author of bestselling book *The Cross and the Switchblade* and founder of Teen Challenge, said this about the church of God in the last days.

> It is going out victorious, with joy unspeakable, riding a river of peace. It is going out in freedom from all bondage, with its foot on Satan's neck. And every member of this true church will live and die without fear. The tempter's power will be broken. Christians will be holy and will tear down idols. They will be just as strong in the Lord as the first Christians (Wilkerson, *The Last Revival*).

Increasing our Faith

It may be hard to believe that we could release glory into the world. "How could we do that? Isn't that Jesus' job? Or maybe his angels?"

Let's not limit ourselves. Believers in Jesus are destined to do seemingly impossible things. We need to believe God. In order to fulfill our calling, we must accept what our calling is. God wants us to become mature revelatory of his glory. Let's be full of faith like Joshua and Caleb, not like the rest of the Israelites who refused to accept their divine destiny.

One problem is that we allow our current experiences to limit our future expectations. We enter the future tied to the past. We lack prophetic unction. We think, "I don't live in much glory now. I'm surrounded by sin, weakness, pain, and suffering. What can *I* do?" We allow our present experiences to limit our spiritual growth.

It is time to break out of limitation. We need to reject wrong mindsets. The word of God shapes the timeline of the world. According to God's eternal word, his glory is going to come. It's going to come through his house - his people. When God's appointed time for something comes, nothing can stop it. We need to get in tune with prophetic reality. Forget slavery in Egypt and adopt the mindset of a conquering nation. You are a son of God now, and the potential to conquer the world is inside you.

- *Points to Ponder* -

1. We are the sons of God by identity, and we have the potential to become the sons of God in practice.

2. We are called to grow into maturity, which means to become like Jesus.

3. When the sons of God are revealed to the world, they will set the creation free from the evil effects of the Fall, and the glory of God will be revealed.

- *Prayer* -

Heavenly Father, thank you for calling me your son. Thank you for adopting me into your family and being my Dad! Help me to rise above limitations and to actually walk as your son in this world. Forgive me for my unbelief. Forgive me for limiting you and for not believing what is possible through your Holy Spirit. I want to grow into maturity. I don't want to remain a baby Christian. I pray that you will help me to grow to fulfill my calling and become the person that you have called me to be. I pray that I would not shrink from the challenge, but that I would be strong in faith, giving glory to you, and believing that what you have called me to do, you will do within and through me. Let everything holding me back be broken and removed from my life. In Jesus' name I pray. Amen.

4

Secrets of Sonship

JESUS REVEALED THE MAIN SECRET of sonship. "The Son can do nothing of himself but what he sees the Father do; for whatever he does, the Son also does in like manner" (John 5:19b).

A son of God lives by revelation from God. He obeys God in everything. He sees God so that he can do God's works. He hears God so he can speak God's words. He has stopped his own works (Hebrews 4:10) and does God's works. He does the works that God ordained for him to do before the foundation of the world (Ephesians 2:10).

A son of God obeys his Father. Where God tells him to go, he goes. What God tells him to do, he does. What God tells him to say, he says.

To walk as God's sons, we must lay aside our own will and do God's will. We must come into a place of inability without God, where we are unable to do anything apart from him. God must be our life. God's sons are being prepared to do nothing except what God tells them to do. They will be strictly confined to God's will, and they will be precise in their lives and ministry. Through obedience, they will become channels through which God can flow into the world.

Obedience is the secret of genuine spiritual power. It causes God's presence and power to break out into the earth. Anytime we want to experience more of God, we need to embrace more of his word. If we want to walk as the sons of God, we must obey him in all things like Jesus did.

> Obedience is the secret of genuine spiritual power.

We need revelation. We need to know what God is saying now.

This is why Jesus said, "man shall not live by bread alone, but by every word that proceeds from the mouth of God" (Matthew 4:4b). When we obey God's word, we eat it, and then we can live by God's power on the earth.

Francis Schaeffer, the American Christian thinker, said, "thank God for the reality for which we were created, a moment-by-moment communication with God himself" (Francis Schaeffer, *True Spirituality*). This communion with God, when it is practiced to its full extent, will enable us to walk as the sons of God, as heavenly people that represent our Father to the world.

Obedience and revelation are intertwined. Obeying God depends on receiving revelation from God, and receiving revelation depends on obeying prior instructions from God. This is an ongoing, ever-increasing process that happens as we learn to walk in the Spirit, read the Bible, pray, stay in fellowship with other believers, and keep trusting God's grace and mercy.

Radical Obedience

Jesus obeyed his Father, even unto death. God is looking for other sons who will do the same.

> Let this mind be in you which was also in Christ Jesus, who, being in the form of God, did not think equality with God was a prize to be grasped for, but made himself of no reputation, and took upon him

the form of a servant, and was made in the likeness of men. (Greek, Philippians 2:5-7)

The sons of God will be humble. Like Jesus, they will learn obedience by the things they suffer (Hebrews 5:8).

They will be willing to have power and not use it,
have glory but lay it aside,
be able to conquer death but still yield to it.

The sons of God will have legions of angels at their disposal, but like Jesus, they will be willing to not call for them (see Matthew 26:53).

They will be obedient to God even if it leads to their own death.

Standing Before God

Jesus walked in heaven, even though he was walking on the earth. He described himself as "the son of man who is in heaven" (John 3:13b). From his spiritual position in heaven, he lived and moved on the earth in his body. This heavenly position is why he walked in spiritual power over the world.

Elijah was another powerful man who lived in heaven. He described God as "the God, before whom I stand."

(e.g. 1 Kings 17:1) Elijah walked on earth in his body while his spirit was before the throne room of God. Heaven was the ultimate reality for him. When he interacted with people on the earth, it was out from the spiritual reality of heaven.

The sons of God will learn to walk in heavenly places. They will be in the Spirit before God's throne. They will stand in the presence of God, even while they live upon the earth.

God gave a powerful promise to Joshua, the high priest, who rebuilt God's temple after the Babylonian captivity. God said Joshua would walk in heavenly places, in authority over the earth.

> Thus says the Lord of hosts, If you will walk in my ways, and if you will keep my command, then you shall also judge my house, and likewise have charge of my courts; I will give you places to walk among these who stand here. (Zechariah 3:7)

God told Joshua that if he was faithful in rebuilding God's house according to God's standard, he would be able to walk in the heavens, among the angels. His heavenly position would translate into authority upon the earth.

It will be similar for the sons of God at the end of the age.

Maturity Through Biblical Church

As we have seen, Jesus compares the church to a wheat plant. In this plant, there are many grains of wheat. These wheat grains symbolize the sons of God. In the natural, the wheat grains mature because the wheat plant matures, so in the spiritual, the sons of God mature as the church matures.

> For the earth yields crops by itself: first the blade, then the head, after that the full grain in the head. But when the grain ripens, immediately he puts in the sickle, because the harvest has come (Mark 4:28-29).

We must labor now to rebuild God's church according to his word. When the church is rebuilt, the sons of God will be empowered with authority over the earth.

We need Biblical church. Many groups that call themselves churches today are not churches according to God. As DNA defines the healthy growth of a plant, so God's word defines the healthy growth of the church. We need to get back to God's plans for the church, dedicating ourselves to the restoration of true New Testament Christianity as modeled in early Acts. When the church obeys the Bible, then she will grow as God intends.

The true church is "the pillar and ground of the truth" (1 Timothy 3:15). The church supports us in our pursuit of God and encourages us to do God's works. When we are part of a Biblical church, will we be able to fulfill our individual callings?

When the plant is mature in the field, the grains will mature. As the church grows into maturity according to the word of God, so the sons of God will grow into maturity. When the grains become mature, it's harvest time.

Harvest time will happen at the end of the age. Psalm 72 speaks of how these mature grains (the sons) will be on top of the mountains. This symbolizes being in a place of authority over the earth.

There will be an abundance of grain in the earth,
On top of the mountains;
Its fruit shall wave like Lebanon;
And those of the city shall flourish like grass of the earth.
His name shall endure forever;
His name shall continue as long as the sun.
And men shall be blessed in Him;

All nations shall call Him blessed.
Blessed be the Lord God, the God of Israel,
Who only does wondrous things!
And blessed be His glorious name forever!
And let the whole earth be filled with His glory.

Ps. 72:16-19

- *Points to Ponder* -

1. The secret of spiritual power is obedience to God.

2. To obey God, we need to conform to the Bible, and we need to hear God's voice.

3. Disobedience is never worth it. It saps us of spiritual strength and blessing.

4. When we obey God, we receive spiritual authority.

5. We must focus on building a Biblical church, for we will only be able to grow into full maturity as a part of a Biblical church.

- *Prayer* -

Dear God, help me to walk as Jesus walked. Thank you that you are working within me to bring me to the im-

age of your Son. I believe that you will finish what you began within me. The distance I have already come on this journey is only by your grace, and your grace will lead me all the way. Help me understand the Bible more. Give me a hunger for your word. Help me hear your voice more clearly. Help me to walk according to your Spirit. Thank you for your Holy Spirit who is my strength to live according to your word. Forgive me for the times that I have disobeyed you. Bring me into fellowship with like-minded believers who will spur me on to greater devotion to you, that we may grow together into the church you want your people to become. In Jesus' name I pray. Amen.

5

Attaining the Resurrection of the Dead

THE APOSTLE PAUL was seeking to grow spiritually. Even though he was a powerful apostle who wrote much of the New Testament, he knew he hadn't "arrived." Paul never settled. He always wanted more of God.

Paul said he was seeking to "know Him and the power of His resurrection, and the fellowship of His sufferings, being conformed to His death, if, by any means, I may attain to the resurrection from the dead" (Philippians 3:10-11).

Paul was trying to attain "the resurrection from the dead." This was a clear destination in his mind, and this great goal motivated him to keep moving forward spiritually.

What does "attaining the resurrection of the dead" mean?

In the next verses, Paul described how he pressed toward this grand goal:

> Not that I have already attained, or am already perfected; but I press on, that I may lay hold of that for which Christ Jesus has also laid hold of me. Brethren, I do not count myself to have apprehended; but one thing I do, forgetting those things which are behind and reaching forward to those things which are ahead, I press toward the goal for the prize of the upward call of God in Christ Jesus. (Philippians 3:12-14)

Trying to attain the resurrection of the dead doesn't mean that Paul was trying to gain the promise of future resurrection. Paul, like every other believer, had already been guaranteed future resurrection when he trusted in Jesus and was born again.

Paul was certainly not struggling to receive assurance of his salvation. Nor was Paul trying to die and be resurrected - obviously, Paul wasn't seeking to die.

The fact that Paul was pressing toward the goal of attaining the resurrection of the dead while he was still alive means that "the resurrection of the dead" is something attainable in this life.

Paul defines "attaining the resurrection of the dead" as becoming mature (or *perfect - teleios*).

In other words, Paul wanted to become a fully mature Christian. He wanted to become a fully mature grain of wheat. He wanted to be revealed to the world as a son of God.

Paul was a mighty apostle who planted many churches, explained powerful mysteries, worked amazing miracles, and wrote much of the New Testament. He wasn't just sitting back waiting for Jesus to come. He wasn't waiting for some sort of bolt out of the blue to transform his life. He was purposely moving forward toward a defined spiritual goal, straining to reach the glorious prize of Christian maturity. He was seeking to be manifested as a son of God.

Paul says this glorious goal of Christian maturity is for all believers.

"Therefore let us, as many as are mature [*teleios*], have this mind; and if in anything you think otherwise, God will reveal even this to you" (Philippians 3:15).

If we are going to become mature (or perfect), we need to have the same mind that Paul had. We must be willing to leave behind what holds us back and press onward toward this goal.

Why did Paul call Christian maturity the "resurrection of the dead?" Maybe it's because the full maturity of believers will happen at the last trumpet and coincide with the resurrection of the dead in Christ. Or maybe it's because coming into full spiritual maturity means to conquer every enemy including death itself. Whatever the reason Paul uses this phrase, it's an important way that God describes Christian maturity.

Paul never attained "perfection" or "the resurrection of the dead" during his life. No one has attained this goal since the first century. This means that this goal still remains.

In the end times, Christian maturity will not be attained by a few scattered individuals, but by a group of God's people, probably all over the world. This event is going to astound the world.

When the sons of God are revealed, the age will be over.

Although God alone knows when this awesome event will happen, we don't need to just sit around waiting for it. We can hasten the arrival of this day as we submit ourselves to God with prophetic urgency, "looking for and hastening the coming of the day of God" (2 Peter 3:12a).

Hymenaeus and Philetus

These teachings about the mature sons of God are not to be handled carelessly. These are the deep things of the Lord. Peter warned us that some things in Paul's letters were hard to understand (2 Peter 3:16). We must not be spiritually rambunctious with such awesome truths.

It is very easy to develop false teachings based on the truth of the manifestation of the sons of God.

Hymenaeus and Philetus were two men that seemed to have misused this teaching. They taught "that the resurrection is already past; and they overthrow the faith of some" (2 Timothy 2:18b).

These men were probably not teaching that the final resurrection had happened and Jesus had returned, for such a claim would have been easily rejected. Instead, they were probably teaching that they had already attained what Paul referred to as "the resurrection of the dead" in Philippians 3. They were telling others they had reached maturity or perfection. They were claiming to be revealed sons of God.

To claim to be a mature son of God without actually having received the fullness of the Holy Spirit is dangerous. Paul says such false teaching will "spread like cancer" (see 2 Timothy 2:17), ravaging the body of Christ. If someone thinks that he is a mature son of God prior to the full outpouring of the Holy Spirit, he is probably a fool. Worse, he may be a false prophet energized by Satan. There have been examples of such deception throughout history - and such deception will increase in the end times. The only solution for those who claim such things might be for them to be excommunicated from the church (1 Timothy 1:20).

There is a lot of deception that surrounds the deeper doctrines of the Lord. People misuse the powerful truths of God to further their own corrupt ends. They twist the Bible, distort the spiritual gifts and baptism in the Holy Spirit, and misuse the name of Je-

> *People misuse the powerful truths of God to further their own corrupt ends.*

sus. They also twist the truth about the manifestation of the sons of God. This has happened in the past, and it will happen again in the future. To stay free from deception, we must stick to the Word of God, abandon the traditions of men, and listen to the Holy Spirit.

The fullness of glory is coming, but it's not here yet.

Two Signs of the End Times

Two signs will accompany the arrival of the end of the age.

> Let no one deceive you by any means: for that day will not come, unless the falling away comes first, and the man of sin is revealed, the son of perdition. (2 Thessalonians 2:3)

Before the day of the Lord dawns, two events must occur:

(1) Apostasy among God's people
(2) Arrival of the Antichrist

Only after these two events occur will the day of the Lord come.

One of these signs has happened, but not the other. Christian apostasy is here, but the Antichrist has not yet arrived. Until the Antichrist shows up, we can be sure that we are not yet at the end of the age. We have work to do. Let's prepare for Jesus, knowing that we have not yet reached maturity, nor the end of the age.

Transfiguration of Jesus

Once Jesus went up to a mountain with three of his disciples. There he was transfigured, and he was overshadowed with the glory he had before the beginning of the world. His face became shining like the sun, his clothes became white and radiant, and his feet became like brass (Matthew 17:1-2).

Jesus probably felt comfortable getting on his familiar clothes of glory. He had been accustomed to these garments from eternity past.

But Jesus didn't keep his 'glory-suit' on for long. He laid it aside and came down the mountain not as the blazing Son of God but as the humble son of man.

Imagine what would have happened if the Transfiguration scene had ended differently. What if Jesus had *not* laid the glory aside, but had instead walked down the mountain in blazing light?

He would have dominated the world.
No army could have killed him.
No human law could have stopped him.

He would become the new law, the new force, the new government.

He would have become king forever.

And the age would have been over.

There is nothing that can stand against the glory of God. It is the supreme force before which everything else must bow.

Jesus laid aside his glory and came down the mountain as a man so he could go to the cross. The end of the age was delayed so we could participate in its glorious culmination.

Transfiguration Through the Will of God

The word *transfiguration* is *metamorpho* in Greek. It describes Jesus becoming glorious in the mountain as his humanity was swallowed up by his glorious divinity. This word is used only two other times in the New Testament. Both of these times refer to something that will happen to God's people.

The first use of the word *transfiguration* refers to how God's people are transfigured by the renewing of their minds.

> And do not be conformed to this world, but be transformed [transfigured] by the renewing of your

mind, that you may prove what is that good and acceptable and perfect will of God. (Romans 12:2)

God commands us to be transfigured. He tells us we
will be transfigured as we renew our minds by the word
of God. As our minds are renewed, we will increasingly
know God's will. Knowing the will of God is the key to
doing God's will. When we do God's will, we will be
transformed.

This key verse reveals the three levels of the will of God:
the good, the acceptable, and the perfect.

1. The Good Will of God

The first level of the will of God is the *good* will of God.
This is the most fundamental level of God's will. It
means doing good as opposed to doing bad.

2. The Pleasing Will of God

The second level of the will of God is the *acceptable* or
pleasing will of God. This means walking in deeper in-
timacy with God. Abraham was called God's friend
(James 2:23). David was a man after God's own heart
(Acts 13:22). These men pleased God. Enoch also
pleased God— so much so that he ultimately walked off
this earth into another realm with God.

> By faith, Enoch was taken away so that he did not see death, 'and was not found, because God had taken him'; for before he was taken, he had this testimony, that he pleased God. (Hebrews 11:5)

We need faith in order to please God.

> But without faith, it is impossible to please Him, for he who comes to God must believe that He is, and that He is a rewarder of those who diligently seek Him. (Hebrews 11:6)

We please God when we walk and live in the Spirit.

> So then, those who are in the flesh cannot please God. But you are not in the flesh but in the Spirit. (Romans 8:8-9a)

When we have faith in God's word more than we believe the things that we can see, then we please God. When we walk in the Spirit more than in the flesh, then we please God.

3. The Perfect Will of God

The highest level of God's will is the *perfect* will of God. When we attain the knowledge of God's perfect will, we can become mature. The perfect will of God means we become precise in our walk with God, doing only those things that He specifically desires us to do. We go where God wants us to go, do what He wants us to do, and say what He wants us to say. When we know the perfect will of God, we will become mature sons.

When we know God's will, we will be able to do God's will. As we do God's will in increasing measure, we mature in our Christian lives and become changed into the image of Jesus. We will walk as He did.

Transfigured by Seeing the Glory of God

The second use of the word *transfiguration* is found in 2 Corinthians.

> But we all, with unveiled face, beholding as in a mirror the glory of the Lord, are being transformed [transfigured] into the same image from glory to glory, just as by the Spirit of the Lord (2 Corinthians 3:18).

As we behold Jesus, gazing at his beauty and knowing him better, we are transformed into his image. We are transfigured from one degree of glory to a higher degree of glory. As we progress from glory to glory, earning greater and greater spiritual degrees from God's University, we are increasingly qualified to reveal God's glory upon the earth.

When this process of transfiguration culminates, we will become mature. We will be revealed to the world as we actually are spiritually - not merely children of our parents, but the sons and daughters of Almighty God.

- Points to Ponder -

1. One main goal of the Christian life is to become mature upon the earth - to attain the resurrection of the dead.

2. Christian maturity is a calling for every believer.

3. When believers become mature, they will be revealed to the world as the sons of God.

4. We are called to be transfigured into the image of Jesus. We are transfigured by the renewing of our minds so we can know the will of God. We are also transfigured as we see more of Jesus.

- Prayer -

Dear God, please deliver me from all spiritual limitations. I know that the devil wants to keep me down and discourage me from fulfilling your purpose, and I reject those limitations. I confess that with God all things are possible. Praise you, Lord, that you are at work in me to prepare me to be a vessel for your glory. Like Paul, I desire to attain to the resurrection of the dead and become a mature believer upon the earth. Give me faith to believe your word. Help me to understand your will, that I may be transfigured. Help me see more of your glorious Son. In his name I pray. Amen.

6

Present Limitation and Future Fullness

It makes me boil when I think of the power we profess and the utter impotency of our actions....Oh, if I could write it, preach it, say it, paint it, anything at all, if only God's power would become known among us!

Jim Elliot

IT CAN BE CHALLENGING to reconcile the word of God with our current spiritual experience. We are called to do the awesome works of Jesus, but we often don't. We are called to release the glory of God into the world, but we often seem unable to.

We often blame our spiritual inability on sin or lack of faith. We lament our lack of prayer or Bible study.

These *are* factors which limit us. But there's a larger issue.

One primary reason we currently face spiritual limitation is because we do not yet have the fullness of the Holy Spirit.

Firstfruits of the Spirit

Paul says that we currently have "the firstfruits of the Spirit" (Rom. 8:23). The firstfruits are the few fruits that become ripe first before the rest of the crop. When a farmer plucks the firstfruits of an apple tree, he gets only a few apples. Later, when all the apples on the tree are ripe, he gets bushels of apples. The firstfruits of the harvest are limited, but they foretell future blessing.

We have the firstfruits of the Holy Spirit. This means that we experience the Spirit in measure, not in fullness. We speak in tongues and prophesy, but in measure. We experience a few miracles and see glimpses of divine glory, but we don't experience the fullness of the Spirit.

At the end of the age, we will receive the fullness of the Holy Spirit. The fullness of the Spirit will completely dwarf our previous spiritual experience.

It will be like entering the Promised Land.

When the twelve Israelite spies went to see the Promised Land, they brought back a bunch of grapes. It was a big bunch. It was so big that it had to be carried on a pole between two men (Numbers 13:23-24). It was probably like nothing they had ever seen before. For them, this was the firstfruits of the Promised Land. This amazing bunch of grapes was a promise of much more to come. When the Israelites would actually live in the land of Canaan, hundreds, even thousands, of times more bunches of grapes just like this one would be theirs.

It's similar for us now. Maybe we've heard a prophecy from the Lord or experienced a miraculous healing. Maybe we've received super-natural provision from God. These are like a foretaste of our inheritance. But when we enter into the fullness of our

> *We have a foretaste of our divine inheritance. There is much more to come.*

divine inheritance, a much larger reality of God will be ours. Miracles will be in abundance.

Earnest of Spirit

Another symbol for our current experience of the Spirit is the *earnest* (2 Corinthians 1:22 KJV). An earnest is a downpayment. It's a partial payment made for some-thing, promising that the full payment will be made later. When someone makes a downpayment on a house, he promises that he will pay the rest of the amount for the house later. After the full payment is made, the house becomes completely his.

God has given us the Holy Spirit. This is a spiritual downpayment, promising that there is much more of the Holy Spirit to come. When the initial payment is in money, the full payment will be a lot more money. When the initial payment is the Holy Spirit, the full payment will be a lot more of the Holy Spirit.

The earnest of the Spirit transforms us and gives us wonderful strength from God. However, it is only a beginning. The future fullness of the Spirit will be of the same quality as the initial payment, but in much greater quantity.

Spiritual Rain

We usually think of the Lord coming back to Earth in a physical body, and he will indeed come to the Earth as a man. But there's more to it than this. Jesus also will come back to the Earth by his Spirit.

> He shall come down like rain upon the grass before mowing, like showers that water the earth. (Psalm 72:6)

Jesus will come like rain to his people.

> Then shall we know, if we follow on to know the Lord; his going forth is prepared as the morning; and he shall come unto us as the rain, as the latter and former rain unto the earth. (Hosea 6:3 KJV)

The Bible clearly says that the second coming of Christ will be like rain. Like a farmer waits for rain, so we are told to wait for the Lord.

> Therefore be patient, brethren, until the coming of the Lord. See how the farmer waits for the precious fruit of the earth, waiting patiently for it until it receives the early and latter rain. You also be patient. Establish your hearts, for the coming of the Lord is at hand. (James 5:7-8)

Water is a symbol of the Holy Spirit.

> He that believeth on me, as the Scripture has said, 'Out of his belly shall flow rivers of living water.' But this spake he of the Spirit, which they that believe on him should receive. (John 7:38-39a KJV)

As believers, we have the living water of the Holy Spirit inside us. This spiritual water is to flow out from us like rivers.

Rain is water that falls from heaven. It symbolizes the outpouring of the Holy Spirit. When Jesus comes back, there will be a mighty outpouring of the Holy Spirit.

Early and Latter Rain

Ancient Israel was an agricultural society. Two seasonal rains marked their agricultural year.

The *first* yearly rain was known as the *planting rain*. This rain fell at the time the seeds were planted in the fields. It caused them to germinate and start growing.

This first rain represents the initial outpouring of the Holy Spirit that happened in the time of the early church. This outpouring enabled the church to begin growing in the earth.

The *second* rain in ancient Israel was the *latter rain*, also known as the *harvest rain*. This rain came just before harvest to mature the crops and make them ready for reaping.

The latter rain represents the great outpouring of the Holy Spirit that will fall at the end of the age. This rain will perfect the church and bring the fullness of God to his people.

The falling of the latter rain will mark the full harvest of the Spirit. It will be the time when we as believers receive the full payment.

> Be glad then, you children of Zion, and rejoice in the Lord your God; for He has given you the former rain faithfully, and He will cause the rain to come down for you — the former rain, and the latter rain in the first month. (Joel 2:23)

When the latter rain falls, God's people will be saturated with Himself. The upcoming downpour of spiritual rain is called the early and latter rain together because it will be such a mighty outpouring. This outpouring of the Holy Spirit will dwarf any revival that has ever come before. God's people will be transformed.

Bright Clouds

God commands us to pray for the latter rain.

> Ask ye of the Lord rain in the time of the latter rain; so the Lord shall make bright clouds, and give them showers of rain, to everyone grass in the field. (Zechariah 10:1 KJV)

Rain comes from clouds. At the end of the age, as God's people pray for more of the Holy Spirit, the Lord will make bright clouds. These clouds represent true servants of God who are full of the Holy Spirit. These true servants of God will pour out spiritual water, enabling the work of God to progress. True ministry speaks as the oracles of God and ministers in God's power (1 Peter 4:11). True ministers are channels through which God flows. They are clouds that pour out God's rain.

False teachers, on the other hand, are compared to clouds without water who don't have the Spirit of God (see Jude 12).

Releasing the Spirit

The living water of the Holy Spirit is inside us (John 7:38-39). The Holy Spirit flows out from us as we speak the word of God. When we speak, the spirit inside of us is released.

When Moses spoke, the spiritual rain of God fell.

> Let my teaching drop as the rain, my speech distill as the dew, as raindrops on the tender herb, and as showers on the grass (Deuteronomy 32:2).

Job also spoke like rain.

> After my words, they spake not again; and my speech dropped upon them. And they waited for me

as for the rain; and they opened their mouth wide as for the latter rain (Job 29:22-23 KJV).

The coming of the pure word of God is like the falling of rain into the earth.

For as the rain comes down...so shall my word be that goes forth from my mouth (Isaiah 55:10-11).

We can discern the spirit of a prophet by testing what he or she says.

"Whose spirit came from you?" Job asked of his errant friends, whom he rebuked for their faulty conclusions (Job 26:4b). As they spoke, they released a wrong spirit.

We need to speak in such a way that the Lord is released out from us. Our speech should be saturated with the Holy Spirit. This is how Jesus spoke, and it's why his words were spirit and life (see John 6:63). This is how the apostles spoke, which is one reason why the early church was so glorious.

Eventually, there will be a flood of the Holy Spirit coming through the servants of God which will saturate God's people, filling them with himself. There will be a revelation of Jesus through end times ministry that will mature the saints and bring a full manifestation of

Christ to the church. When this happens, the church will be filled with God. The "grains of wheat" will become mature, and the sons of God will be revealed.

> Then the remnant of Jacob shall be in the midst of many peoples, like dew from the Lord, like showers on the grass, that tarry for no man nor wait for the son of men (Micah 5:7).

Light in the Midst of Darkness

The world is about to become very dark. The Antichrist will dominate the world, and Satan will try to destroy God's people. But in the midst of this darkness, spiritual rain will begin to fall.

> Arise, shine, for your light has come, and the glory of the Lord is risen upon you. For, behold, darkness shall cover the earth, and deep darkness the people; but the Lord will arise over you, and his glory will be seen upon you. (Isaiah 60:1-2)

When the spiritual rain falls, it will fall onto God's people. They will be filled with the Holy Spirit. Spiritual light will rise upon them, and the glory of God will be seen through them. The darkness that covers the earth will not be able to overcome this powerful manifestation of light.

David Wilkerson wrote:

> The church is going to experience an undeserved outpouring of love, mercy, and kindness. It is going to come in a time of great affliction, with a tempest raging, with anxiety on all sides, when society is being tossed about. (Wilkerson, *Last Revival*).

As the end times approach, both darkness and light will reach an apex. Let's focus on the light more than the darkness. The glory of God defines the future of the world. Our eschatology should be defined by a strong expectation of God's glory.

The Impact of Glory

When the glory of God comes, everything will change. Imagine the glorious works of Jesus being done all over the world, in every nation and city. Jesus prophesied that his people would do greater works than he did. (John 14:12). The sons of God will walk through the earth, revealing God's glory and power everywhere.

When the latter rain falls and glory breaks forth, the earth is going to be changed. The last will be first, and the first will be last. That which was effective will be made ineffective. The reign of death will end, and life will dominate the world.

The coming manifestation of the glory of God has many implications – political, economic, social, and cultural. The current authority structures in the world will face an end. The emerging New World Order, which is based on empty promises, will fall. God's people are not going to take over the current organizations that rule the world. Instead, these systems will be removed by the Spirit of God. God's kingdom will reign over the world, which will be a completely different government based on righteousness, supernatural ability, and eternal life.

The glory of God all over the world is our goal. Total victory over the darkness of the world is our aim. The eradication of evil and the establishment of God's reign is the end of history. To achieve these awesome things, we must believe in their possibility. We must be willing to launch out in radical faith in God. Remember the words of William Carey: "Expect great things from God. Attempt great things for God." Let's break out of the limitations of unbelief and just go for it. William Carey believed that all nations can be impacted by the gospel, even though very few of his contemporaries believed him. But now, Carey's audacious goal has almost been reached.

> *To achieve awesome things for God, we must first believe they are possible.*

We need to accomplish even more for God. Let's be bold. Let's say right now prophetically that the knowledge of the glory of the Lord will cover the earth as the waters cover the sea. Even if few Christians agree with us now, it's going to happen. Let's be pioneers, not followers. Let's hold onto God, not Christian culture.

We'll have to make strong decisions in order to experience the coming glory. Our cry must be like that of pioneering martyr, Jim Elliot:

> I pray that the Lord might...give you a hallowed dare-devil spirit in lifting the biting sword of Truth, consuming you with a passion that is called by the cultured citizen of Christendom 'fanaticism', but known to God as that saintly madness that led His Son through bloody sweat and hot tears to agony on a rude Cross—and Glory! (Elliot, *Shadow of the Almighty*).

The present age began with Christ as a baby in Bethlehem; it will end in God's glory all over the world. It began with the humble birth of the Son of God; it will conclude with the manifestation of the sons of God.

Let's pray for God's rain. When we long for God and make radical decisions, he will bless us with an outpouring of the Holy Spirit.

"For I will pour water on him who is thirsty, and floods on the dry ground; I will pour My Spirit on your descendants, and My blessing on your offspring" (Isaiah 44:3-4).

- Points to Ponder -

1. One reason we face spiritual limitation is because we don't have the fullness of the Holy Spirit.

2. The outpouring of the Holy Spirit is like rain. At the end of the age, there will be a great outpouring of God's Spirit.

3. During this final outpouring of the Holy Spirit, God's people will receive his fullness.

4. True ministers of God will release the Holy Spirit in increasing measure.

5. The outpouring of the Holy Spirit will cause the glory of God to impact the world, bringing transformation to the whole creation.

6. We must press into this glorious future.

- Prayer -

Dear God, thank you for the wonderful firstfruits of your Spirit. I praise you for the amazing Helper that your Holy Spirit is to me. I would be lost without this precious gift! God, teach me to follow your Spirit more and more, and be increasingly empowered by him. I pray for a great outpouring of your spiritual rain. I pray that you give me the audacity to believe that you will do amazing things. Embolden me to make the radical decisions I need to make in order to see your glory revealed in this world. My life is for your glory. Do with me as you will. In Jesus' name, I pray. Amen.

7

Gideon: Warrior for Glory

When God wants to move a mountain, he does not take a bar of iron, but he takes a little worm. The fact is, we have too much strength. We are not weak enough. It is not our strength that we want. One drop of God's strength is worth more than all the world.

D.L. Moody

THE EVENTS of the Old Testament are recorded for our sakes, to teach us important truths regarding the end of the age.

"Now all these things happened to them as examples, and they were written for our admonition, upon whom the ends of the ages have come" (1 Corinthians 10:11).

The life of Gideon (recorded in Judges 6-8) reveals many truths related to the final manifestation of the glory of God.

Gideon had a low estimation of himself. He was from a poor family and thought he was the least in his father's house. He didn't think he could do much for God. But God had a different view. God said, "God is with you, you mighty man of valor" (Judges 6:12).

God called Gideon to deliver Israel from the army of the Midianites. It was the appointed time, and Gideon was God's chosen man. God delights in taking the foolish things of the world and confounding the wise. He delights in taking the weak things and putting to shame the strong.

We might think that we are too weak to do anything. We might think that it's impossible for people like us to release the glory of God. The solution for our perceived inability is not to focus on ourselves, but to focus on God. His will is going to come to pass, and he is going to accomplish his plans through his people.

Confront False Religion Among God's People

The first thing Gideon had to do was tear down the altar of Baal. He had to confront the old religious order.

Gideon's father, along with many other Israelites, had adopted strange religious prac-

tices which prevented them from experiencing the fullness of God. Empty religion had to be thrown out in order for God to take over.

> *Empty religion must be thrown out in order for God to take over.*

It's similar for us. If we're going to receive the fullness of God, we must abandon empty religion. There are many religious practices in Christianity today that have no basis in the Bible. We must throw these things out. We need to hear and obey Jesus. We need the power and glory of the one true God. The hour of battle is coming! Empty religion will only leave us weak and powerless.

It's not easy to tear down idols. Gideon was afraid to confront the vain religion of his fathers. But he knew that God was calling him to do it. He eventually mustered up enough courage to sneak out at night to the family altar. Under the cloak of darkness, he tore down the idol.

A holy confrontation of false Christian religious practices is necessary for God's people to move forward. Judgment must begin at the house of God (see 1 Peter

4:17). Repentance from false religion prepares the way for glory.

Gideon didn't know what the result of his idol-destruction would be, and he might have feared bad repercussions. But surprisingly, his father was supportive.

God will work miracles when we obey him, and our courageous acts will be the means of others' deliverance.

Confront the World

With that victory under his belt, Gideon began to focus on confronting the Midianites. He was full of doubts about such a huge task, so he put out a fleece. He said, "God, if you're really with me, let the night dew be only on the fleece, but not on the ground."

It happened.

Gideon still doubted, so the next night he said, "Let the dew be only on the ground and not on the fleece."

That happened too.

Slowly, faith began to build in his heart that he might be able to do what God was calling him to do.

Sometimes it takes a while before we believe that God will do what he said. "Oh fools, slow of heart to believe" (Luke 24:25b), said Jesus. We need to keep focusing on God. Keep believing his word. Let's expand our vision of what is possible through the Holy Spirit.

Gideon may have thought, "God, you're so strong, you can just destroy these Midianites. Why do you need me? Aren't your angels up to the task?"

It bears repeating: to get victory in this earth, God works through people. Ever since Adam handed the dominion of the world over to Satan, God uses people to effect redemption. Noah built a boat. Priests offered sacrifices. The Son of God became a man and died on a cross.

Right now, God is looking for faithful people through whom he can work to fulfill his glorious end-times purposes. Through faithful souls, he is going to wrest back his creation from the serpent.

What Adam handed over to the enemy, the sons of God will take back. They will do it through the power of their Captain, Jesus, who has already won it all.

> *What Adam lost, the sons of God will take back.*

The Final March

Gideon decided to go for it.

He blew the trumpet and gathered the people of Israel together. An army joined together and began marching toward the Midianites.

In the end of the age, at the appropriate time, the people of God will respond to the sound of the trumpet. Holy warriors will unite around Jesus.

Gideon had grown spiritually. He was becoming more confident. He was hearing the voice of God, and he was walking according to the commands of heaven. His actions no longer made sense to those around him; maybe they didn't even make sense to himself. But the stronger reality for Gideon was the presence of God. Through obedience to heavenly revelation, Gideon was walking in heavenly places, revealing God's power upon the earth.

All forward progress into the glory of God is based on hearing God's voice and doing what he says. Our own clever ideas will never bring deliverance. They will only bring confusion. We need to follow God's word.

God said to Gideon, "There are too many people with you. Let all those who are fearful go back." Fear will keep us from fulfilling God's plan. We need to conquer fear by walking closely with the Lord. If we can defeat fear, we can defeat Satan.

12,000 people were afraid. They gave up and went back.

Not everyone will be able to fulfill God's glorious plan. For various reasons, many will sit on the sidelines. But there will be a remnant who are willing to grab hold of all that God has for them.

Gideon gathered the remnant and started marching again.

Spiritual Discernment

The army came to a stream of water.

God said, "There are still too many. I want all the glory for myself. I want the victory purely by the power of my Spirit. Let all those who drink from the water of the stream using their hand remain. All who put their face into the stream and suck up the water directly into their mouths can leave."

Only 300 men were left.

Meeting a powerful enemy army with 300 people who drank water in a certain way makes little sense according to the natural mind, but Gideon had stopped eating from the tree of the knowledge of good and evil. He laid down his own reasonings at the foot of God's throne. He listened to the Lord and did what God said. His army was being honed by the wise counsels of Almighty God.

Drinking water by hand instead of sucking it directly from the stream represents the need for discernment. Sucking up water directly from the stream might cause someone to swallow impurities, for he is just drinking whatever comes into his mouth. But someone drinking from his hands has a chance to check what he's drinking first to make sure it's pure. This shows discernment. This also reveals alertness. The ones bowing down and drinking are not aware of what is happening around them. Their heads are down, and they are just focused on satisfying their thirst. But someone drinking using his hand has his head up. He will not be caught unaware by the enemy.

There is a lot of spiritual activity in the earth today, and much of it is not from God. As we approach the end of the age, dangerous spiritual activity will increase. Evil spirits are entering the church, masquerading as the Holy Spirit (2 Corinthians 11:14). False prophets are arising, and lying miracles are happening.

We need discernment. We can't just accept everything that comes to us by supernatural means, assuming that every miracle is from God. We need to be sure that our spiritual drink is the pure water of the Holy Spirit.

The remnant army of 300 kept going forward, onward toward the Midianites.

God was preparing the way before them. He had begun putting fear in the hearts of their enemies. The Midianites began murmuring about the mighty warrior Gideon and the powerful army of God. They knew they were about to be defeated, and they could do nothing to stop it.

Victory

God told Gideon's army to take torches, trumpets, and clay pots to cover their torches. These three things don't look like weapons, but they were God's chosen means of releasing his power.

In the middle of the night, armed only with pots, lights, and trumpets, Gideon surrounded the camp of the Midianites.

Suddenly, they blew their trumpets and shouted, "The sword of the Lord and of Gideon!"

The noise struck the sleeping Midianites like an alarm. The Israelites smashed the clay pots covering the torches. The light blazed forth as the sound of the trumpets pierced the night air. The Midianites were defeated by their own ensuing confusion, and the power of God overthrew them.

The Israelites conquered a vast army through the spiritual power of obedience to God.

The weapons of Gideon's army are significant. The torch represents the Holy Spirit, which is the light of God inside us. The clay pot represents the outer man (2 Corinthians 4:7) in which this treasure rests. The trumpet represents the clear word of God coming through his prophets.

In the end of the age— at midnight, when it is dark and there is no time left— through the breaking of the outer man and radical obedience to Jesus, the Spirit of God will be released from his people. Christ in us, the hope of glory, the glory in potential; will become Christ through us, the manifestation of glory, the glory revealed. The glory of

> Christ in us, the hope of glory, will become Christ through us, the manifestation of glory.

God will break out from us into the world, and God will take over.

. . .

The appointed time is rapidly approaching. God is preparing radical hearts for a full revelation of himself.

Light is breaking forth, and eyes are being opened. Through new vision, there are new possibilities. The Promised Land is coming into view. At the same time, giants are appearing on the horizon. Clouds of darkness are swirling. Evil is being unleashed. The great battle of the ages is almost upon us. There will be a great war in the spiritual realm – between light and darkness, good and evil.

Armageddon will be a spiritual battle fought all over the world. The forces of darkness will come against the children of God.

The time is approaching. Swords are being sharpened. Faith is rising. Radical, sacrificial obedience is paving the way for glory. Victory in the name of Jesus is about to be revealed. The glory of God will be released by those wielding the sword of the Lord.

With man it is impossible, but not with God. With God all things are possible.

The children of light will prevail through the power of the Holy Spirit. God's glory will be revealed - not in a partial measure, not in fleeting glimpses in a corner of the world - but as a sustained, powerful, continual, overcoming, conquering revelation of God. The great prophecy that sways the future is about to be fulfilled: "the earth shall be filled with the knowledge of the glory of the Lord, as the waters cover the sea" (Hab. 2:14). This will happen through God's faithful people, wherever they are, all over the world. Everywhere, a new order of the glory of God will prevail.

Now is the time for the culmination of all things. Let doubts dispel, and faith arise. Now is the time to begin walking as Jesus walked. Now is the time for the Spirit of Christ inside of us to break out from us and show the world that Jesus Christ is Lord.

> For it is written, As I live, says the Lord, every knee shall bow to me, and every tongue shall confess to God (Romans 14:11).

> That at the name of Jesus every knee should bow, of those in heaven, and those on earth, and those under the earth, and that every tongue should confess

that Jesus Christ is Lord, to the glory of God the Father (Philippians 2:10-11).

When Jesus is exalted, God is glorified. The more Jesus is exalted, the more God is glorified. At the end of the age, Jesus will be exalted over all, and his glory will be all over the world. The glory is coming because Jesus is coming, and nothing will be able to stop it.

- Points to Ponder -

1. Our spiritual ability is not determined by ourselves, but by God.

2. To move forward into God's fullness, we must throw out empty religion.

3. If God has called us to do something, he will do it. As we look to him, fear will leave.

4. To release the glory of God, we must have discernment.

5. The final manifestation of God's glory will be through the breaking of the outer man (bearing the cross and obedience), and a firm declaration of the word of God.

- Prayer -

Heavenly Father, thank you for the boldness of Gideon. Give me boldness. Help me trust in you and not in myself. I know that you have called me to do things that are beyond my own abilities. Help me walk by your Spirit and do those things. Win victories through me. Prevail over your enemies through me. Though the battle be intense, Christ has already won, and I praise you for his victory. Let the earth be filled with your glory and praise! In Jesus' name I pray. Amen.

CLIMB

by Amy Carmichael

A voice said, "Climb." And he said, "How shall I climb? The mountains are so steep that I cannot climb."

The voice said, "Climb or die."

He said, "But how? I see no way up those steep ascents. This that is asked is too hard for me."

The voice said, "Climb, or perish; soul and body of thee, mind and spirit of thee. There is no second chance for any son of man. Climb or die."

Then he remembered that he had read in the books of the bravest climbers on the hills of the earth that sometimes they were aware of the presence of a companion on the mountains who was not one of the earthly party of climbers.

And he remembered a word in the Book of Mountaineers... it heartened him, for it told him that he was created to walk in precarious places, not on the easy levels of life.

A Very Present Help: Life Messages of Great Christians

Contact

Visit

www.bethelcornerstone.org

More books by Peter John Brooks:

Seven Foundations

Spiritual Technology

Three Marys

Kingdom Explosion

Goat Tags

Absurd Christianity